and then

and then

BY TIM NOLAN

n
RIVERS
e
PRESS
w
MSUM

First Edition
Library of Congress Control Number: 2011942068
ISBN: 978-0-89823-265-3
American Poetry Series

Cover design by Allen Sheets
The cover photograph was taken by Tim Nolan on his cell phone camera (an old Motorola Razr cell phone) in July 2009 from the cemetery at Fort Abraham Lincoln, Mandan, North Dakota.
Author photo by Scott Streble
Interior design by Daniel A. Shudlick

The publication of *And Then* is made possible by the generous support of the McKnight Foundation and other contributors to New Rivers Press.

New Rivers Press is a nonprofit literary press associated with Minnesota State University Moorhead.

n RIVERS e PRESS w MSUM

New Rivers Press
c/o MSUM
1104 7th Avenue South
Moorhead, MN 56563
www.newriverspress.com

For my parents
Marge and Pat Nolan

We don't need sugar, flour, or rice
or anything else. We just want to see
our dear ones.

—Hafiz

contents

I.

And remember, no matter where you go,
there you are.

—Confucious

At the River

In my city I walk
through the woods

and lean against an old
elm tree and watch

the foggy dusk and watch
the lights across the river

and the birds—they are in
their own world, which nobody

but me notices right now
someone burns wood

in a stove to keep off
the last of the winter

I am careful walking
down the iced paths

to the river because men
sometimes fall in

as I lean back against
the solid elm tree

I think of Jesus with his
spine the way he hung

from that tree and came
to love how he was held

by the embrace of that tree
from which he hung

a man could fall in
if not careful near the river

the birds what friends I ignore
the way the birds watch

from above as I walk
and turn down the path

I amuse them—I am below
as they fly to the trees above

Late Night/Early Morning

It's the time when my heart
jumps to my throat

It's the time of the gloom
of Walt Whitman

Or the despair
of Emily Dickinson

Nobody wants to record
these minutes

It's anyone's
overnight dread

Anyone's night sweats
anyone's turning over

This can happen in early
spring or at the height

Of summer the birds
wild in their nests

The sense that it could all
crash in at any moment

As well as the small perception
that the light has already changed

The Kids

At work during the day
your old pictures
on my window ledge

Various stages
of the various *yous*
each one of the *yous*

The three of *yous*
holding signs that say
Happy . . . Father's . . . Day

It's one of those moments
that could slay me
if I let it

Your eyes those years ago
remain the same
for each of you

Isn't this *The Iliad*
as well as *The Odyssey*
the heroic past?

It's everything this snapshot
all the king's ransom
all the privileges of the realm

He's Become So Little

My Dad with his big soft eyes
has entered that frail zone

his bones stick out on his back
when I go to hug him (he's

so little) *My Dad* was never
little he was always six feet

185 pounds now he's five foot
eight 135 pounds (he's so

little) he's almost a talisman
of himself *(My Dad)* hanging

from my neck so I can remember
him years from now but

he's still here (he's so little)
he's still him. How did he get

to be this way? Did I forget?
Some years I must have forgotten.

Her Chin

She is speaking from the edge—
her head is tilted up—I want

her to have some water—I say
Mom you should have some

water—she trusts me—we
speak the same language—both

of us are at some edge—then—
I notice her chin—how her words

are spoken upside down as if
she were speaking to me across

a rushing river—she's tired now—
her words run out—her chin

defiant—the skin of her neck soft

Driving

I pick you up to go
for a drive

you never say no
usually we orbit

Lake Harriet the sun
on your face

once you took me
downtown on a bus

that was years ago
I wore short pants

I wanted to be older
you wanted that too

now I buy you a glazed
chocolate-covered doughnut

we drive toward the sun
along Minnehaha Parkway

You are happy with the doughnut
this makes me happy too

The Desire to Quantify

How much would be
enough?

How many shadows?
How many trees?

It's good you have
ten sufficient toes.

You might want
even more.

How many hours
and days?

You really want
just a few

of those infinite
days

or those sprawling
nights

of blasted stars.
Turns out

You don't need much.
Just a few.

Tanned Old Man

In a *Speedo* collapsing
slowly upon himself
in the sand he resembles
Cormac McCarthy but I doubt
it's him now he looks
more like Burt Reynolds
in that centerfold if Burt
Reynolds did that now
all these old people
not that I'm not *there*
more or less old women
with pierced navels *God*
is good and has retired
to some place with sun
where he can do
little harm

Palm

The green sea the blue
sky the glamorous royal
palm with a cluster
of coconuts the intentions
I've always had the
suspicion that nothing
is a matter of intention
the accident of arrival
at this age or any age
being basically *me* all
these years the sand
that has been and is being
created by the pull
of the moon from quartz
boulders to marble cities
just look at the white
sand spreading everywhere
as evidence of how long
time is *just a glimpse*
we get just a few snapshots
to send to you *the swaying*
of the royal palm tree

Gorgeous

Gorgeous the sun
and the clouds
and the blowing air

Gorgeous the pine tree
the pink wall
the faded chair

Gorgeous my bare knee
my old shoes
my blue ink

Gorgeous and too much
the breath, the hot dog,
the sharp mustard

You my dear, are most
gorgeous your hazel
eyes, your brow

As you read
the paper *what news*
reflecting on your face

Wind

At the end of the day
summer
everything is directed
by the sun

The wind is just the effect of
the warming of the air,
etc., and somehow
the turning of the sun

Of course it is breath
the wind
the divine breath
and ours as well

How it clears
the mind
the wind
through the window

Or here sitting
out in the wind
where if I had a hat
it might fly off

As the top of my
head has seemed to
the wind entering
all the emptied space

In Her Small Room

There are snapshots
of our faces
reassuring to see

There's the low-slung bed
a dresser—pastel
landscapes screwed to the wall

Nothing extra except
the extra bed
for the person not there

We sit on the edge
of the extra bed
pretending this is just

A normal visit—nothing
is normal anymore
she's mad and far away

She tires of us
she says so making it
much easier to leave

My Mother Says the Word *Fuck*

Impossible to imagine
like a lamb suddenly growling

If you knew her at all
you would never believe

she could even shape
those sounds in her mouth.

She's forgotten many words
but this one she remembers–

fuck–reportedly she said it
in anger to a gentle Somali aide

who has been very good to her.
It's not enough to say–*Oh, what*

mysteries there are!–fuck that.
Or–*one must bear one's cross*–

no one cares to explain
exactly how she used the word

fuck whether she combined it
with *you* or if she called

someone *a fucker*–could not,
she could not have said

mother fucker–she could not
have called down that curse

being herself a mother most of all.
It might have been *fuck you*

or even *fuck me* or most
probably *fuck everything*

this fucking world this
beautiful fucking world

Since

Weeks seem months
or years
since that day

That marked day
in early June
day of bells and lights

Precise machines
checked the beat
and flow and temperature

Of you becoming
not-you slowly
your face composed itself

To reach this open note
since everything
led to this

The Dead

Are silent yet noisy

Still yet active

They go about their business

Which is to have no business

Their days are the same

As their nights

They speak with no voice

They journey while staying

They are always on the threshold

About to speak or dream

About to come back

They are forever waiting

They are passive-aggressive

They should be committed

They should finally decide

Where they are—not to mention—

Where they will finally be

Sunday Morning

So many mistakes pile up
  it's difficult to sort them
Who has the time?
Should have locked in the rate
Should have bought skim instead of 2%
The kids arrived only to leave in a huff
When you (that would be me)
  look at yourself in the mirror
It is with this weariness
Oh–it's you (me) *again*
A song bird singing a tiny grooming song
  just shit on the little table
He missed my glass of iced coffee
Thankfully
I would like to throttle
  the sweating man on TV
Who says *Jesus* in two desperate syllables

Jesus would say—

Grow up—take a deep breath

My faith (is it yours?)

To be stupid and available

In this—the best of all possible worlds

Beautiful Day

The wind with this *out-of-nowhere*
urgency—the clouds floating above
as prairie mountains

The great blue dome—this long
memory—could be forgetfulness
coming back as long memory

We are at the apex of twelve noon
a sudden coolness in the air
a turning toward and a turning away

The siren call of the cicadas
the fresh smell of cut branches
the old mud nest falling to the grass

The wind blowing up inside
the linden tree—all the swaying
of the sun in this mottled shade

II.

In fact every poem
might be called "Moment."

—Wislawa Szymborska

Those Moments

When Walt Whitman caught the eye
of a passing teamster or when Neruda

reached down to pick up a purple shell
when James Joyce watched the Irish Sea

and watched the girl in her fluttering dress
dancing on the strand when Wallace Stevens

glanced from the black Buick and saw
the deer upon the white hillside or

when Louise Glück imagined the Greeks
their arms more golden on the shores of Troy

when Shakespeare momentarily placed himself
on a cobbled street at the center of Verona

when Doctor Williams or Doctor Chekhov
crossed the precise threshold of contagion

when Allen Ginsberg shuffled toward home
down East 12th Street a North African sky above

when Elizabeth Bishop observed that rainbow
that pooling rainbow of gasoline on the still water

or when Lincoln turned the mule at the end
of the furrow and turned toward

the unlikely harvest of himself and Emily Dickinson
struck her dash at the end of the line when

Sappho chanted: *Here now the delicate Graces*
and the Muses with beautiful hair

First Hot Days

On these first hot days
I always think of the dead

how they endured the heat
in their heavy woolen pants

and long skirts. How they all
wore hats even in the heat

the men taking out straw hats
when it got hot and the dust

the dust on hot days
reminds me of the dead. The dust

could be theirs, their own dust.
How they endured the dust

after they endured the mud
and the horse shit that was

everywhere. Before they were dead
didn't they feel the way I do?

The heat and the sun
and the dust on heavy boots

it was too much for this life
too much of this life.

Then as the evening came on
as they unbuttoned their shirts

unclasped their heavy stockings
this cool breeze through the window

through the lilacs enough
to go on enough to go forward.

19th Century Deaths

At Fort Abraham Lincoln
seven miles south

of Mandan, North Dakota,
they died in the fall and winter

of 1876 from asphyxia
as a result of intoxication

suicide by opium gun-shot
wounds self-inflicted

and accidental frozen
to death typhoid fever

diphtheria shot by civilian
shot by self shot by

unidentified person frozen
to death by self by self

giving up in the fast snow
frozen to despair the harsh

northern plains the deep
snow intoxication leading

to gunplay somebody said
something somebody said

nothing despair in the wide
open landscape the despair

of the survivors of
The Last Stand some of them

died from their wounds
shot by Crazy Horse shot

by Gall shot by unidentified
Cheyenne some of them

giving up on the plan for
triumph some of them

Irish giving up on the new
world all of them loose

with themselves so to speak
their lives loose some

of them survived until 1933
or 1945 never forgetting

how the Indian Wars ended
never forgetting the power

brought to bear as they died
out in the open in the fast snow

My Grandfather's Way

He had the best American voice I know
the short and rapid-fire dead pan
the not-expecting-much
surprises that might come around the corner
the urban Irish ghetto let me tell you
semi-con job about to turn into
a story involving a herring choker
a kraut and a kike
the way he swallowed his words as he said them
the way he didn't expect much from words
simple home-made tools
the cheap beer the cheap seats
the pickled herring brown mustard
Wolf Bros. sweet rum-soaked cigar box
scores and the papers the morning *Tribune*
and the evening *Star* folded in his lap
the smoke curling from his lips
the clipped practical nine innings
keep track of each ball and strike
sharp pencil moments defined with a check mark
the passing time
cut the grass hang the shirt out on the line
read the running obituaries
recall the War keep track of the dead
young faces in the basement
the battalion photograph a black dot
of ink on the khaki tunic the summer
baseball Halsey Hall Herb Carneal radio
pragmatic clear channel impact
of his voice the sad funny boring melancholy
not his word of the long years without her
the way he would speak to women differently
than the way he would speak to me

one of the boys in the neighborhood
one of the boys on the troop ship crossing
the pond the way he would speak to women
surprising how tender he could be
when said and done all added up

The Soviet Sears Store

On Lake Street was the center
of the known universe in 1959

You could buy a house in pieces
or chocolate stars displayed in those

Slanting glass cases or a vacuum cleaner
that would spin a beach ball

As large as Jupiter—all those
blending colors—and tools to fix

Anything—a ladder to climb
the side of the house and we came

In our cars down Lake Street
to be there on Saturday morning

To be busy buying whatever—popcorn—
or a refrigerator—we were rapacious

In our buying power our desire
to get ahead or keep up—

It was our cathedral built
in the collective style of the times

Just at the same time missiles
were pointed at us centered on Honeywell

A few blocks away where they made
something that centered our missiles on them

We didn't know anything except the sound
of popcorn popping like small arms fire

The Sadness of Eisenhower

That day in January 1961—he stood hatless
a white scarf around his neck—the wind
sharp and blowing—it was black and white

I felt bad for him—I didn't want him
to go—his ordinary voice—
the cranky up and down of it.

The wind was bracing—he seemed sad
as if he had failed—maybe
he had failed—at what? I didn't know.

I was too young to know anything—
the black and white of it—the bright sun—
the sharp cold—it was time for him to go.

Fever

In those days
of tonsillitis
my fever shot up

I thought my mother's
hand would fly off
as she shook the thermometer

The little bulb
of mercury spiked
in the red zone

I didn't notice
my chattering teeth
my mother noticed

Put in the bathtub
put *me* in the bathtub
in a shallow pool

Of freezing water
scrawny boy–barely there
She yanked the handles

Of those ice cube trays
the cubes struck
the porcelain like dull diamonds

Shivering and burning
I tried to talk about something
with the few words I had

I was there—I wasn't there—
her face—she—
I could see how worried

How you look into
someone's eyes and see
It was as if—*it was—*

That I was being carried
toward Paradise
in a litter pulled by a camel

Paradise that dense valley
below the presiding
mountain

The mountain being my pillow
Paradise being this cool
breeze through the window

Marlon Brando in Tahiti

Talking on his ham radio
to someone on the West Coast

of Africa—he doesn't tell them
he's Marlon Brando—they talk

about the bugs of Africa
and Tahiti—how the mosquitoes

in Tahiti have yellow stripes—
and the mosquitoes in Africa

have orange stripes—nothing
is missed by Marlon Brando—

he talks to many people—they
never know they're talking

to Marlon Brando—just some guy
in the South Pacific—At night—

Marlon Brando walks along the shore
of his island—the moon is full

like a white melon—the flies
swarm in front of his face—

the face of Marlon Brando—
we already know his face—

and how he will turn his face—
looking up toward the moon—

Words Can Describe

Did you ever think the astronauts should have done
a better job describing the moon for the rest of us?

We spent billions of dollars to send them there,
to walk around on that glassy sand in those

synthetic mukluk boots, driving their goofy, lunar
dune buggies, slapping a golf ball 5,386 yards

to an endless sand trap. We heard that static through
corridors of space until they had the chance to describe

exactly, ROGER, what they saw, AFFIRMATIVE,
and instead we heard: "Words can't describe,"

CHECK, "the stark beauty," A-OKAY,
"of the landscape . . . I mean the moonscape."

They were young. Inarticulate. Absolutely
without words to describe what they saw. But then,

when they watched the earthrise from the moon's
fluorescent horizon, I remember, their words were pure

excitement and *Oh, my God* and *It's so beautiful.*
We knew what they meant from our earth-bound

imaginations. We knew that the rising earth was
the jewel of our breathing, the swirling of our weather,

a wondrous cat's eye marble rolling across black velvet,
reminding us of our daughters' faces, the freckled

continents, those oceans of blue eyes, the determined set
of our son's jaw in the angle of a peninsula. And that stillness

around the globe like a lake viewed through the pine woods.
They were speechless because they were reminded of *everything*

they missed. From their tin-foil shed, on the Sea of Tranquility,
first witnessing, ROGER, the beloved's face out there.

Cuba

I want to go to Cuba where the cars
float in the 1950s where I sometimes

float in that combination of fear
and floating as if in a big blue Chevy

floating right through my childhood.
I don't care what anyone says

I've always had some fondness
for Fidel Castro. It seems to me he

was always thinking of his country
and his people even when I listened

on my transistor radio to the sinister
broadcast from Cuba 1967 a woman

talking about *Child Care Centers*
I was sitting on my front stoop

the ear piece in my ear and the dusk falling
her broken English *how outrageous*

Child Care Centers as if I knew
a thing about the coming revolution.

Old Astronauts

When they get together now—
they nod to one another—

don't talk about the pitch
black of airless space—

don't want to remember
the dust of the moon

in the treads of their boots—
they fall in bathrooms—

just like everyone else—
but from a greater height—

and before their heads
hit the tiled floor—

they float for awhile—
weightless seeming to dance

at the end of a cord—
one of them found

Noah's Ark—or is just
about to—mostly they

remain dead silent—
whatever they saw and felt—

lost for generations—it's that
they were led to believe

they really could escape—
the pull of the molten core

Clo-Spin Laundry

I remember carrying that giant green
laundry bag on my back trudging

down St. Clair to the Clo-Spin
Laundry in a sudden snow storm

sidewalks filling up with snow
streetlamps glowing as I spilled

into the warm and friendly confines
of the Clo-Spin Laundry all by myself

with everything we owned in terms
of clothes agitating there in the hot

water while the snow fell outside
with rushing urgency

and the big dryer drum turning
like a great paddlewheel mixing up

everything from our tender lives
my sensible khaki work shirts your

bras and panties the red-striped
cotton socks I wore with those heavy

work boots and wild zebra sheets
we bought at Montgomery Wards.

How did I get stuck in the rinse cycle?
Stuck in the permanent press setting?

I could have stayed there forever
spinning in the never-ending orbit

of the Clo-Spin Laundry happy to be
in a city where time would go on and on

Picasso

How can we believe he did it—
every day—for all those years?

We remember how the musicians
gathered for him—and the prostitutes

arranged themselves the way he wanted—
and even the helmeted monkeys

with their little toy car cerebella—
posed—and the fish on the plate

remained after he ate the fish—
Bones—What do we do with this

life?—except announce: *Joy.*
Joy. Joy—from the lead—

to the oil—to the stretch of bright
canvas—stretched—to the end of it all.

Big Tree

We set down our lawn chairs
and watched this agile man

in the boom crane bucket
work his way up among the limbs

like an earnest lover—he marked
his fall points with ropes and pulleys—

and it was interesting and sad—
to have the oldest elm on the block

brought down—it's changed
the whole climate in our little place—

which is our place—and our tree—
we all call him—*Big Tree*—everyone

knows who he is—his great twisted
limbs—reaching up in an easy arch—

what does it matter—what does it
matter how we watch and wait—

for this low thud of the huge limb—
the way it shakes the light away?

What I Missed

Everything—the East Village
1981—missed the Gem Spa—

missed the Fillmore East—
missed Allen Ginsberg—Patti

Smith—missed heroin—missed
gay bondage sex—which did

take place upstairs—we could hear
Greg—the sex—or the instructions

involving—*putting something here*
while I can move over there—

missed all of the bohemian possibilities—
missed the mark—I suppose—

If I told everyone what I was
doing—everyone would only say—

boring—did not miss you—somehow—
I did not miss you—remember

how the cats would wail from
the backyard—the Ginkgo trees—

in that hour of awakening—
when we would turn toward

each other?—we would turn
over in our sleep toward

each other—while *The Cat Lady*
called in her strays—

the clattering pie tins—*oh dear—*
Oh, My Dear—I found you—

Off Gramercy Park

I'm walking down the sidewalk
rolling Maeve's empty red suitcase
that contains her empty black

suitcase—they had both contained
her clothes and special shampoo
and her laptop which draws

her in like the Oracle at Delphi—
I just dropped her off
at her dorm on East 12th Street

and now I'm wandering like Odysseus—
not really—I'm wandering like
myself—down the streets I once

knew—*what do I know about*
anything—makes sense that I
should look up and see that sign—

Pete's Tavern—Made Famous
by O. *Henry*—since I've just fallen
out of an O. Henry story—where—

It's all so sad—not really—
Odysseus didn't think of it
as *sad*—

It's just this wandering—
the way there's always a twist
right when the story seems to end—

III.

to be with each other in silent unspeakable memories

—George Eliot

Something Happened

When he almost died that night
under the glaring hospital lights

she stood off in the corner, *she was*
herself she would have been fine

if he died that night, we were all
ready for it to happen then it didn't

And he came back to himself not
remembering anything about his

struggles. *They happened in a dream.*
She couldn't stand the up and down of it.

Something happened *can we say this?*
Something happened when he came back.

Son

Except when he sleeps, I never
get to see the crown of his head.
He always wears a baseball cap.

His jeans hang low off his hips.
This is the fashion. He holds
his hands—as I do—as all the men

in our family hold their hands—shyly.
He's a beautiful boy—smart.
The two of us—we cannot say this

directly—we can only indirectly
acknowledge how beautiful and smart
we are through our mutual

admiration society where we speak
in nods and grunts and mumbles
from the crowns of our beautiful heads.

Pod Hotel, NYC

We have bunk beds—Frank
on the top watching his own

individual LCD TV tuned
to *Baseball Tonight*—while I

watch *New York 1*—a show
about a tapas bar in Tribeca—

There is no room to turn
around—I crash my head

on the aluminum slats above
I'm falling asleep to *Baseball*

Tonight—the spectacular
catch—the endless green

lawn—I'm falling asleep
beneath my son—*he's breathing*—

and intently watching the white
ball on the green lawn—

We are both breathing—
in the family crypt—

he's awake—*I'm asleep*—
this—is the way it will be—

Cleaning My Uncle's Gutters

He mentioned it a few weeks ago
he never thinks about such things.
The leaves in the gutters they

got along fine without him
but now he wants to get this done
before the snow and ice.

So he's up at the corner
reading the *New York Times*
and I'm dragging a ladder

around his house up and down
scooping pigeon poop out of the gutters
along with the briny leaves

and the crumbled twigs. I did not
disturb the nests of the dumb blue
blank-eyed pigeons up under

the eaves in their cozy coops.
My hands ache from the cold water.
I try to unplug the downspouts

and down goes the water like whiskey
down to the center of the earth.
I'm not saying this to have you

think *he's a nice boy* it's that
so much is left undone. Cleaning the gutters
pleases me more than he can know.

Father's Day

Strange not to be able to call
to call you collect from some

long distance to say I'm thinking
of you. So instead I call Mom

and get your voice repeating
with great care the number

I've just called and as you say
Please leave a message

I can think of nothing in words
words only go so far

from voice-box to eardrum when
I need other means smoke signals

a solar flare the exact pitch
of my breath somehow sent out there

Breaking Up the Household

He's gone for good—she's away—
We take apart the marriage bed,
        the grandfather clock, the shelf with books
We put away the dinner dishes, the souvenir
        spoons, the egg timer shaped like a hen
We gather the random papers,
the church bulletin, the clipped article

Nothing seems to matter much
No thing stands out with the pulse of them—
No love letters, no confessions written in blue ink—

The slender scissors he used to open letters
The green Connemara marble shaped like a petrified egg
It's all too much—the weight of slips of paper—the weight
        of the casual words there—
The way the slips of paper could be scattered in a small wind

The place in the thriller novel where he stopped reading—

We put everything in boxes with tight lids

The lids are meant to quiet the voices for now–

Just for now–their voices seem to be quiet–

Dad

I have become him
for mine

As he is gone it must be
I continue

At least for awhile
until someone else

Will be *him*.
It's not just a way station—

This turning over—
he was a definite—*he*—

Himself—himself alone—
just like me

I wouldn't burden
anyone with being—*him*—

It's just that someone
must—

Pine Cones

I know about pine cones
from the Norway pine out front

I've picked up thousands of pine cones
fresh green pine cones compact and hard

as hand grenades or the dry
blossomed pine cones weighted to land

upright they sit out in the lawn
like miniature versions of the old tree

I sit under. I've filled hundreds
of plastic garbage bags with pine cones

I've been hit in the head many times
by pine cones–it's not so bad–

pine cones–could be worse–could be
coconuts could be some kind of tragedy

what I can't figure out not one Norway pine
sapling despite all the seeds not one

example of the next generation in the spread
of the tree no offspring. Makes me think

what loneliness there is in the old tree
at the same time *what excess.* How much

devotion can be paid to pine cones?
This one for example sitting upright on the arm

of my wicker chair curled wooden petals
exploded from those dark and ancient folds.

Smelt

I only have them once a year
when they are running up North
on Lake Superior their season

is so brief. I get the blue
plate special at Peter's Grill
deep-fried *headless* smelt

I eat the scales and fins and bones
along with tartar sauce, a fat roll,
coleslaw, hash browns.

It's probably not healthy, but once
a year to celebrate the end
of May, why not? I eat the whole

plate of smelt, dipping them in tartar sauce,
crunching their tiny bones, almost
enrolling in *The School of Smelt.*

Entering their mass migration, the home
river, the icy water, the long sun
their flashing, silvery, slipping sense.

Grocery Receipt

That served as a bookmark
a few pages in—Jorge Luis Borges'

Labyrinths—it's from Pathmark
of Weehawken #178. You spent

$16.89, gave them a twenty,
got back $3.11, on 9/20/82,

(*twenty-eight years*) not even a whole
meal—cigs ($7.40) (must have been

a carton), something called
"APPETIZING"—for only 89¢

(what could that have been?)
Scott Towels, ice cream, an apple,

Martinson Coffee, Planter's Peanuts.
What were you thinking?

Peanuts, cigarettes, coffee, ice
cream, an apple—towels—to wipe up

the mess, and "APPETIZING"
(for only 89¢), must be

"APPETIZING" has gone way up
in price, beating everything else

in inflationary terms. Must be
the best bargain you, or any other

Borges, ever made. Walking
home, do you remember

eating that apple—*dreaming*—
of opening up the jar/bottle/canister

of "APPETIZING," sitting
down at the desk/table/counter

eating/drinking/smelling it,
like any other animal, *desiring* it all?

Small Words

I love the small words
then and *now* and *once.*
How do they say so much? *Yet*
and *because,* not to mention,
and—I love how *and* becomes
the *stars* the *moon* the *wind.*
And what about *if?* You could
write a treatise on *if.* You might
lisp on *if.* But it would send you
off to the speculative realm.
And *was* and *is* and *has been*—
these are mere conditions of timing,
something for the *tense masters.*
While *frog* and *goat* and *roast*
belong to the real place—the *grit,*
the *shit,* the *sand,* as the fires
bank low, as the *wind,* as the *stars* rise.

Yellow Chrysanthemums

These must have been the royal
flowers of the Chinese emperors.

How do we deserve them now
in white planters near the front door?

All these yellow blossoms packed
in a mound. When I come home

Yellow chrysanthemums light the walk
while birds fly in circles overhead.

Bread

Making it is an investment in the future
when you can spread the butter
on the warm inner naves of this cathedral

and offer a slice to your daughter
who says *Yes!*—accepting it
without question, as she plays

the piano. *Bread* is always
a welcomed interruption from nothing,
but your own life and your own

going on. As you fill your gut,
you think—*it's really a great*
puffed up cumulus cloud following

you in the blue sky above. There is
no ulterior motive to bread, other than
growth—from the yeast, to the smile

of your daughter, to the breaking off
of the heel, which you love best,
the rounded end, the way it comes around.

Hand

I love the way we shake hands
or kiss them or hold them

down the path. It's all there,
the span of our hands, the wide

world. The way we can hide
from everything, cover our eyes

with our hands. The little moons
rising above the cuticle, the palm–

Hand it over–Give me your hand–
I have to hand it to you–

The hand with its deep rivers,
its lifelines to the edge of *this* life–

Thanksgiving

Thanks for the Italian chestnuts—with their
tough shells—the smooth chocolaty
skin of them—thanks for the boiling water—

itself a miracle and a mystery—
thanks for the seasoned sauce pan
and the old wooden spoon—and all

the neglected instruments in the drawer—
the garlic crusher—the bent paring knife—
the apple slicer that creates six

perfect wedges out of the crisp Haralson—
thanks for the humming radio—thanks
for the program on the radio

about the guy who was a cross-dresser—
but his wife forgave him—and he
ended up almost dying from leukemia—

(and you could tell his wife loved him
entirely—it was in her deliberate voice)—
thanks for the brined turkey—

the size of a big baby—thanks—
for the departed head of the turkey—
the present neck—the giblets

(whatever they are)—wrapped up as
small gifts inside the cavern of the ribs—
thanks—thanks—thanks—for the candles

lit on the table—the dried twigs—
the autumn leaves in the blue Chinese vase—
thanks—for the faces—*our faces*—in this low light.

IV.

Perhaps the truth depends on a walk around the lake.

—Wallace Stevens

I Find Myself

Sitting by myself with my notebook—
and you dear listener—as though
I could be Emily Dickinson speaking
to the world from my corner room

Upstairs in Amherst. And all the hymns
are in me—those gestures toward God
or the spider weaving its web
in solid quatrains. Our minds desire

The right angles and almost nothing is
as it seems—for instance—these words—
moving through your mind—*dear reader*—
can make you realize you love this world.

All Souls' Day

Coming home at dusk—the moon—
bright and fat with mountains
and craters and endless gray sand—

All of it lit white and dimpled
in the darkening sky—makes me
remember the souls I've known—

Somehow they sing together—
through the cold air—
from the distances—from great

Distances they sing—yet it seems
so close after all—the way
they sing directly into my ear—

It's beautiful how they sing—
the old souls—the way
they know the whole song—

Isn't it Something?

How the snow falls slowly tonight
and fills the sidewalks

while Louis Armstrong and the Hot
Five play *Savoy Blues*

and the snow finds its
perfect accompaniment

isn't it something how my
scribbled note (this very note here)

can be my own just as the pure
goofy joy of Louis Armstrong's

trumpet tone *his easy tone*
all the way from 1927

to right now *right now*
in this moment of falling snow

The Thread

The other morning I sat on the edge
of the bed like an old man

Trying to thread a needle in the low
morning light to sew

A button onto my coat. Who
makes these needles with

Sub-atomic eyes? Meanwhile
the fat brown thread, which I chose,

Is a frayed and fat mess
which I've licked into

A smeared and frayed and fat
and fucked-up mess. I just

Want a button on my coat
and now my frustrated hands

Begin to tremble—*what's this?*
What a fucked-up-button-fucked

Life I lead. I just want
a button on my fucking coat.

Who's supposed to be in charge
of buttons and needles? So I end up

With a securely-sewn button
that doesn't go through

The fucking button hole. *What*
a fucked-up life I live.

How fucked up is this?
I can't button my fucking coat.

New Year's

I resolve to get a handle on my
                    personal matters, including my weight

which I will increase this year
                    with the Krispy Kreme diet which

all the celebrities are trying out, ballooning
                    up in Malibu so they can float

like fat kites above the beach.
                    And money—I will spend it all

without worry, down to the last cent,
                    the final zero on the bank statement.

Then, I'll borrow to go to the movies,
                    buy that 40-foot mobile home, the boat,

buy the spare boat for those days
                    in the summer when I don't

want to use the regular boat.
                    And smoking—I'm going to switch

to Gauloises or Players' Cuts or
                    Camel Straights. I have not been

smoking enough, and I spend
                    too much time between cigarettes.

This year, I will light them
                    one from another and be in a cloud

of beautiful blue smoke from Winter
into Spring when all the buds come out,

right through Summer and Fall
when we used to burn the leaves

in the gutters, and we thought of
those ceremonial deaths with the souls

rising like incense to the blue sky.
This year, whenever I think of doing

something nice, think of buying flowers
for my wife or a little china tea set

for my daughters or a Hank Aaron
baseball card for my son, something

I know they will like, I'll think
better of it and buy something for myself,

Something to go with the spare boat—
a depth finder—so I can watch the school

of fish below in a sonar cluster, the way
the Northern Pike looks like a bold dash

on the screen, and I will be so
happy floating on the choppy lake,

alone with myself, fat and content,
smoking, might as well have a beer

or one of those little airline bottles
                    of Crème de Menthe, tasting like cough

syrup, so I shake my head
                    as if to clear my mind, but my mind

cannot be cleared of the daily thought,
                    the constant belief that I'm having

the year of my life, the abandoned year,
                    the careless year, the one that can't be

touched, the year that must generate
                    all those new and hopeful resolutions.

Cold Night

My feet are cold the car
is cold the car sounds
like a bucket of bolts

Rolling down a hill
it's so cold that my breath
falls like ice from the roof

And the dog tip-toes
on the sidewalk and the lake
seems to breathe deeply

Just as it freezes solid
and the crisp snow under the tires
sounds like brown paper bags

Crumpled in a garbage can
everything is cold even the stars
they crack in the dark blue

Long Winter

So much I've forgotten
the grass

the birds
the close insects

the shoot—*the drip*—
the spray of the sprinkler

freckles—strawberries—
the heat of the sun

the impossible
humidity

the flush of your face
so much

the high noon
the high grass

the patio ice cubes
the barbeque

the buzz of them—
the insects

the weeds—*the dear*
weeds—that grow

like alien life forms—
all *Dr. Seussy* and odd—

here we go again—
we are turning around

again—this will all
happen over again—

and again—*it will*—

What I'm Meant to Do

Linger in hardware stores
among the male and female
electrical plugs unfold

a napkin in my lap as the plate
is presented before me
smoke a Cuban cigar

that makes me dizzy, take
the bus to the end of the line
only to find it's not far enough

sit in front of Rembrandt's *Lucretia*
until I am Lucretia
inhabiting her sorrow, fall

asleep in the comfortable chair
the little volume open the last
words entering my dream

speak for the insignificant
memory the one we all know
the light in early spring the way

the child we were comes back
goes to the dentist to personally
cancel the appointment, then

that sense of endless possibility
you know that luxuriant wasteful
sense of possibility in spring

And Then

We were talking about Death—
as if it were some program
on the History Channel—Lizzie said:

"Here's my nightmare—my soul
doesn't go anywhere—it stays
in that box—I'm all alone with myself."

I said that was really depressing—
I told her she shouldn't think that way—
as if I had some control over it.

Together—we were depressing each other
completely—just talking about Death
caused this terrible claustrophobia.

She said "Sorry"—but I could tell
she wasn't sorry—because she was
smiling—in that special way she has—

smiling from her brow to her chin—
What will happen?—What will happen?—
She was smiling—*she knows*—I have no idea.

Speaking for the Inner Life

The *Inner Life* is a shy shoe salesman
might have a special interest in women's feet
might not want to speak out loud in a group

The *Inner Life* would never remember
that the gas gauge was on empty
the *Inner Life* would walk a long way back

The *Inner Life* cries easily when anyone else
is brought to tears it is this automatic
empathy that makes the *Inner Life—inner—*

The *Inner Life* is without skin meaning
you can't be certain whether the *Inner Life*
is in the room with you or somewhere else by itself

We know the *Inner Life* is fleeing across
America while its cousin the *Outer Life—*
never acknowledges their relation

The *Inner Life* would like to speak up
there is so much to say about dreams
for example that innermost sanctuary of

The *Inner Life*. But let's face it no one
wants to listen to someone else's dreams
the urge toward interruption is almost civil

The *Inner Life* can be as heroic as a dying animal
a cat struggling to get to the litter box across
the room even when its legs will not work that way.

Message

I wanted to send this message
to you just so you would know

I was thinking of you at a time
today when the wide world crashed in

but I should not say that in my message
that would be upsetting to you

and serve no purpose other than to give you
an opportunity to send a message to me.

Did you know that Vincent Van Gogh
could send a letter from Arles in the morning

to his brother Theo in Paris who would
send a letter back arriving the next day?

(Who says things have changed for the better?)
And the money would arrive from Theo

to buy a wicker chair rough pottery
a visit to the prostitute for *hygienic purposes*

a meal or two at the little café on the square
and paint fat tubes of paint

enough yellows and reds and blues to cover
a field or to animate the friendly face

of the uniformed postmaster Roulin. I wanted
to send this message to you about

nothing except I was thinking of you
and I wanted you to be sure of that.

Today

I made lots of noise and smoke cutting the grass—I washed
some dishes—I watched part of a baseball game and part
of the news—I saw the maple seed pods helicopter down
from the tree next door—I thought about Constantine Cavafy
waiting for the barbarians—I read some poems by
Wallace Stevens—I entered into his processional voice—
I drove a few places—avoiding pot holes—I wondered when
I might be able to replace the shock absorbers on my car—
I read the first part of a biography of Mickey Mantle—
I didn't know how much pain he suffered or that he wet
his bed every night until he was in the minor leagues—I saw
Maeve backing down the driveway in our red car
which needs a new transmission—I puttered around the house—
I thought about all the dead people I know—as if they were
right here with me—they seemed to be—I thought about my
death—how when it gets here—the cars will be long gone—
my death will arrive in a big Yellow Checker cab—the driver
from Pakistan—somebody I don't know yet sitting in the jump seat—

Oriental Rug

We are the family
that has an oriental rug
in our garage—because

It was my grandma's rug
bought in 1924—machine-made
not worth anything—

But I can't throw it out—
so it's in the garage—the rug
I walked on as a child—

Through the looping vines—
the deep red background that
spoke to our common blood—

Now it's in the garage—
we drive in on the rug—
eventually—we will throw it

Out—or the rug will throw
itself out—or it will simply
fly away—just as she did—

The Light in the Corner

I'm alone in the house at night
hardly ever happens

The TV is a blank face
with a dull surface

Everything is quiet except
the airflow from the furnace

The light in the corner
of the next room

I'm drawn to it
there's a table mismatched

Chairs a lace tablecloth
like a wedding dress

There's a vase of dried flowers
everything's quiet

Any speech at this point
would be mine

But I'm quiet—I'm listening
for the sound coming from the light

On Water

The Styrofoam cup of it on the table
beside the bed a straw sticking out

The last drop of it sand in the canteen
you must have seen that movie

The slapping of it against those smooth
green rocks at the edge of the northern lake

The crashing of it on the Steel Pier
in Atlantic City during a strange hurricane

The frozen armies of it floating down
like paratroopers landing on the sidewalk

How it desires to head south in spring
rushing through the opened locks at the Falls

The intensity of its love for gravity
its love for transforming itself

The way it wantonly slops over the edge
of the metal pail while at once

It exhibits discipline urging itself up
through copper pipes to reach the second floor

Its warmth as we sink each day
into the contented bath of it

And then dry ourselves off as if
in refusal of it as the dog

Shakes himself off at the front door
as if to be finally rid of it

The noise of it that is the dog's
lingual communion with it *in the red bowl*

The warm rubbery taste of it from
the green garden hose—the outrageous

Quenching of thirst of it—the iron pump—
the cold rusting coming forth of it

The question it raises of where we
begin and where it ends or the other way

Our containment of it our ingestion
of it our sweating off of it

The into and out of our cells of it
across the membranes of our cells

The obviousness of it *of course*
and its obvious mystery the solid of it

Skating across the clear lake on this sheet
of glass that somehow illuminates the deep

The humidity of it the emptying of it
from the de-humidifier the pulling

Of it out of the air the breath
of it on a summer day the way

We breathe it in and drink it in
and fall to the ground in the wet grass

And turn our faces up toward it
and watch the puffy clouds of it

The medium of it within which
we are capable of speech

The sliding syllables of it not
to mention the vowels and consonants

Of it the way it is the lubricant
of everything the way it wants

Nothing in return except to be
itself as it turns into something

Else turns into ice cream or
turns into wine or turns into

The sweet breath/drink/bath of it
we just took into ourselves

The sip of it through the flexible straw
that is leaning now in the Styrofoam cup

Me, Myself, & I

I find myself in that sweet
meadow of myself among
a bleating flock *turns out*
I'm the shepherd of the events
of my life and I wonder
how did I ever survive
to become this accumulation of me
this silent acceptance like a lake
just above the freezing point
there's a swimmer in the lake
turns out it's me swimming across

Sketch

Here I have my notebook

I could draw a house
in the valley with a curl of smoke

I could draw a skyscraper
with windows that don't open

Or an airplane with a pilot's
face staring off toward his horizon

I could say something important
or nothing important

I think *the nothing important*
matters the most

Several people in the next room
begin to laugh loudly

In this sketch I will not go
to join them *in real life I did*

In this sketch I stay here with you
as if we were at a deathbed

We cannot tell if the death
belongs to me or to you

In any event the death is right here
as the people in the next room laugh

Do you feel a tenderness toward
how silly they are and how alive?

Like a parent you want the best for them

They are in the next room *laughing*
we are here *wondering*

What stupid thing made them laugh?
How it matters now most of all

Acknowledgments

I want to thank the editors of the following publications where many of these poems first appeared, sometimes in different form:

American Life In Poetry: "Picasso"
Bellevue Literary Review: "Something Happened"
Flurry: "The Sadness of Eisenhower" and "New Year's"
Green Blade: "Pine Cones"
Great River Review: "First Hot Days," "Those Moments," "19th Century Deaths," and "My Grandfather's Way"
Kinship of Rivers, www.kinshipofrivers.org: "At the River"
Knockout: "And Then"
Legal Studies Forum: "Words Can Describe"
motionpoems.com: "Old Astronauts" was animated in 2009 by Emma Burghardt.
The New Republic: "Son"
Saint Paul Almanac, 2010: "Clo-Spin Laundry"
Saint Paul Almanac, 2011: "Cold Night"
Sleet Magazine: "At the River," "Driving," "Gorgeous," "Palm," and "Tanned Old Man"
The Sun Shines, The Day is On: Poems of Gratitude: "Thanksgiving"
Turtle Quarterly: "Bread" and "Message"
Water~Stone: "Old Astronauts," "Picasso, " and "Speaking for the Inner Life."
What Light: Minnesota Artists Online, www.mnartists.org: "Cuba" and "What I'm Meant to Do"
The Writer's Almanac: "Long Winter"
Your Daily Poem, www.yourdailypoem.com: "Words Can Describe"
Zebra Film Festival, Berlin: "Old Astronauts" was shown at the Festival in October 2010.

I thank my wife, Kate; our kids, Elizabeth, Maeve, and Frank; my many pals in poetry who have read and listened to these poems over the years and given me so much support and encouragement—Joyce Sutphen, Connie Wanek, Patricia Kirkpatrick, Garrison Keillor, Jim

Moore, Carol Connolly, Phebe Hanson, Michael Dennis Browne, Robert Hedin, James Elkins, Phil Bryant, Henri Cole, Todd Boss, James Silas Rogers, Greg Watson, Kimberly Nightingale, Brett Ortler, Katrina Vandenberg, Wang Ping, Sharon Chmielarz, Kirsten Dierking, Liz Weir, Regan Palmer, George Bilgere, Louis Jenkins, Pam Vander Wiel, Ann Burns, Nell Mathews, Greg Weyandt, and so many other great friends.

Finally, great thanks and appreciation to Al Davis and everyone at New Rivers Press for taking on another book of mine. In 2008 when New Rivers accepted my first book, *The Sound of It*, I was almost at the point of giving up on publishing a book at all. Thanks Al and New Rivers Press for reviving me.

Author Biography

Tim Nolan received a B.A. in English from the University of Minnesota and an M.F.A from Columbia University. He graduated from William Mitchell College of Law and is an attorney in Minneapolis.

During his time at Columbia, Nolan was the managing editor of *Columbia: A Magazine of Poetry & Prose*, and for five years he was the primary poetry reader for *The Paris Review*. He has been writing poems for nearly forty years, and his work has been published or is forthcoming in national publications including *The Gettysburg Review, The Nation, The New Republic,* and *Ploughshares.*

Garrison Keillor has read several of Nolan's poems on the National Public Radio program, *The Writer's Almanac*, and the former United States Poet Laureate Ted Kooser selected Nolan's poems for *American Life in Poetry.* New Rivers Press published Nolan's first book of poems, *The Sound of It*—a Minnesota Voices Project winner—in 2008. *The Sound of It* was a finalist for the Minnesota Book Award in Poetry in 2009.